NARROW CRADLE

NARROW CRADLE

wade kearley

BREAKWATER
P.O. Box 2188, St. John's, NL, Canada, A1C 6E6
WWW.BREAKWATERBOOKS.COM

A CIP catalogue record for this book is available from Library and Archives Canada

ISBN 978-1-55081-815-4

We acknowledge the support of the Canada Council for the Arts. We acknowledge the financial support of the Government of Canada and the Government of Newfoundland and Labrador through the Department of Business, Tourism, Culture and Rural Development for our publishing activities.

PRINTED AND BOUND IN CANADA.

Canada Council for the Arts Conseil des arts du Canada

Canada

Newfoundland Labrador

Breakwater Books is committed to choosing papers and materials for our books that help to protect our environment. To this end, this book is printed on a recycled paper and other controlled sources that are certified by the Forest Stewardship Council®.

To Katherine, as always,
to our daughters Julie and Sasha,
and to our grandchildren Luke and Annika,
who have helped us broaden our
understanding of love and deepened
our appreciation for the all-too-fleeting
time we have together.

And to Paul Bowdring, wherever he may be.

ACKNOWLEDGMENTS

Thank you to my editor and friend Kevin Pittman. Thanks also to those friends and family who read some of these poems and offered encouragement: Paul Bowdring, Alison Dyer, Geoff Kearley, Paul Kearley, Tonya Kearley-Russell, Cynthia O'Toole, and Gordon Rodgers. A big thank you to Tamsyn Russell, who embraced the challenge to write the music for "Amy Chains," and to Kelly Russell, who assisted in the final arrangement. Thanks also to James Langer and to Rebecca Rose for welcoming me into the Breakwater family. And lastly, thanks to those friends and acquaintances who allowed me to use their words as the starting point for poems including "—suicide wings," "–in between," "—undone," "high anxiety in redhead cove," "—american goldfinch," "—re: the last one in the sequence," and "—on the road to mount abu."

Several of these poems are revisions of earlier work, including "—deciduous" and "—mother's day revisited" from *Let Me Burn Like This* (Killick) as well as "—postcard from under a bridge," "—postcard from the hills above clarenville," and "—postcard from the holiday inn" from *The People's Road* (Harry Cuff).

"If self is a location, so is love:
Bearings taken, markings, cardinal points,
Options, obstinacies, dug heels, and distance,
Here and there and now and then, a stance."

FROM "The Aerodrome"
Seamus Heaney, *District and Circle* (2006)

CONTENTS

December on Lawlor's Brook

Hide your face from blame, cover your wrists,
Your scars accuse me of your bloodletting.
At this dark solstice I recall dandelion twists,
Cicada hopscotch, dancing, you forgetting
Breakfast to linger feline in the grass.
Found, a four-leaf clover, the lucky luck,
Then skipping past the corner boy's passes,
To Mrs. Burry's stoop. Trade for a quarter.
I blame you, hiding behind sad clown eyes
That innocence and beauty, making me despise
What you've become. And yet, what could you do
But hold the constant blade that routs your demons?
My calls to heal yourself are empty sermons
Designed to hide my fatal fear of loving you.

—bar-headed geese

On a winter migration out of the Himalayas,
After drinking a free rye or two too many,
I am beating my way past screen-flickered faces
when the seatbelt signs blink and the floor falls away.

My shoulder collides with an overhead bin and I sprawl
into your lap. You question how I knew you were lonely.
With the pain in my arm, I ignore your smirk,
take the seat beside you, signal for another drink.

I confess to you that, *After six months at an ashram,*
I ran out of patience. Now I just want to get home.
A slight nod and you turn to the window, the setting sun,
point to a wavering line of geese winging their way
on a river of air through mountains that prowl the sky.

You turn green eyes on me, indulge in a yawn, and manage,
How is it that up here. . . where it takes ten breaths. . .
to equal one on the ocean. . . these geese can still fly?
I wave the drink away and, after you glide into sleep,
clutch at the headrest, struggle to rise to my feet.

—rue

"If self is a location, so is love"
Seamus Heaney

With hours to kill before my snowbound flight, I watch the same street from the same cafe where, outbound, was it just six months ago? I last saw you, my daughter. Time falls away and I am there again. Gazing down at the sidewalk three storeys below the rim of my cup, I see a minstrel plunk a black box on the concrete near the corner of Peel and Sainte-Catherine. She crouches briefly to plug in her guitar as the human flood eddies. She sets her top hat down to catch donations, then flicks back matted hair to stare skyward. As she strums, her body starts to sway. People stand in a small knot around her, some toss coins or tuck bills into the hat. Up here I keep my change. The murmur of travellers and the clink of cups calms me into believing I belong.

I tell myself I travel light, *My suitcase holds no regret.* But then up the sidewalk you come dancing in time with the musician who opens her arms for your embrace. You scoop her collection into your purse and pull her hat over your head. I stand at the window, knock the glass with flat hands, upsetting the coffee chatter.

Don't leave me! Don't leave me! Before I can gather my things to run after you, you hail a cab, turn with the sun on your cheek, duck into the car and pull away without looking up.

The sidewalks are shadow now.   The musicians flown. No one
lingers on the corner. I see   a stranger in a greatcoat,   her
hair loosely shawled. She drags   a fir tree wrong end round
on a small blue sled. My heart   beats in time with her
footsteps.   She stops as if remembering an errand,   looks up,
waves a mittened hand.   I almost wave back.

—suicide wings

I still wish I could tell heaven from hell.
Your room abandoned for more than a year,
but I know some part of you lingers here.
My skin electric when I open the door,
see the duvet twisted, clothes left to burn.

I can't pretend that straight has no bends.
All those years listening outside as you thrashed
in your room, panic mounting as pain crashed
over you, pressed your face into the floor,
while outside I stood frozen, nowhere to turn.

I couldn't tell your anger from your cries for help.
There was no magic pill. No magic wand,
and as hard as I tried, no magic words
to stop the demons at your shoulder,
from grafting broken wings to your bones.

Is there a gate between self-love and self-hate?
I used to wish you could fly,
soar over the many who never looked in your eyes.
But then, when you couldn't take it anymore,
you climbed the carpark stairs, threw yourself at the sun.

I've been told when you were young you were old.
And where are you now? Is it heaven or hell?
You stepped away from your pain and you're still
out of reach. Maybe we're even on that score?
But now I haunt the space where you came undone.

—prayer rock

The twin-fisted rock on my work table,   a nugget of peridotite
forged   twelve miles deep,   shoved surfaceward from the
molten core   when continents collided.   Buried for millions
of years under alpine mountains, scoured by glaciers and
finally exposed   on a ferric mountainside   a lizard-skin
tableland   weathered by rains and ice,   it defied lichens
and moss.

Seconds before I hiked into range,   this iridescent rock
yielded   to the heave of frost   forsaking balance for
the conviction   of gravity, tumbled   over the
long-fallen scree,   bounded over crowberry, lupine
rebounded through dwarf birch   hurtling over guardrails.

Far below, I stumbled   over decisions that displaced my
serenity,   children grown and fled, my relationships
shattered. Then I was plunging headlong   into doubt over
troubles yet to come.   I was lost in time when   it struck
my foot,   recalled me from the exile of thought   to this
impossible   connection   eons in the making.

If the stone had been larger   it might   have fractured bones
but instead   only staggered me   my ankle bruised through
the boot.   The stone felt as heavy as solitude.   I shoved it
in my backpack,   lugged it home.

I ponder the rock on my work table   and when thoughts
intrude   I sometimes take its rough geometry   in my
hand, marvel at embedded gems   and the precision of the
journey   that brought us here   from the universe before
the universe that started with a bang.

—in between

found poem in an email from Kevin

Xmas come and gone,
New Year's Eve next.
No plans for me.
Stone Jug restaurant is having a do,
but expensive,
and I don't know people going.

All good so far.
No resolutions, per se.
I sent an email
to Mariza
and proposed.
I am awaiting her reply.

NPR website has a listing
of 300+ "best books" of 2016.
Two are poetry.

But I just learned of this Jarmusch film:
http://www.npr.org/2016/12/27/507125816/
paterson-a-love-poem-to-poetry-from-director-jim-jarmusch

I must see that one.

I'm at the Stone Jug for a beer.
I must get home and see
if Mariza has replied...

January on Lawlor's Brook

I gun the car where the sign says, "Blind Hill,"
And plunge weightless into the pit of my gut.
At the bottom, a stop sign. I recall
How nothing's possible anymore; I'm caught
In your wreckage at sixteen as you drove,
Pregnant and scared, crashed with my fifty years
Into the frozen brook beside the road,
Me fumbling for a grip, your mother in tears.
Now I wonder, "What have you denied me?"
Did my heart forsake too soon its journey?
Do I need foreign cafes for scribbling?
Just when I felt like my life was drifting,
You anchored me with a grandchild, then another,
Taught me there are many ways to mother.

—love doll

Poised here in the window   with plastic snow collecting
around my boots, I keep myself relaxed   watching shovellers
shovel   a path to the steps, and though the hour is late,   they
usher revellers revelling   into the darkened shop.

In here, under the glitter of my night sky,   the guests grow
louder, break into slurred melodies,   casually rehearse their
infidelities.   They are oblivious to the blue and red flashing
in the street.   A cop, big as a bear,   cups his paws over his
eyes,   strokes our faces with a flashlight.

Someone grabs me from behind   and lugs me up the stairs
past a crowd huddled near the washroom   watching as
my ex-husband   guzzles a beer while pissing   into the
ice-jammed toilet.   I don't need anyone to take me back now,
no matter how talented they were.

I don't feel the cold   here, propped against the railing   I
don't need silence.   But if I could move, I'd hand it all
back, the rags,   the fur,   the flesh,   not caring who owns
what,   and escort them out the doors.   The knocking
downstairs gets louder, so some genius cranks the music.

Then I see her   in front of the long mirror.   Over her
shoulder her eyes break on me.   I want to reach for her.
She lists towards me, catches on a corner.   Her eyes are
painted,   her bare shoulder patched.   She doesn't need
warmth. Her skin is smooth plaster.   I'm grateful my
reflection   is the woman on her other arm.

I try to talk, and she pauses,   so we both pretend to listen,
but hear nothing,   not even the roar of the party talk   until
the door glass crashes to the floor.   The cop pushes past,
clamps cuffs on my ex's leg,   drags him into the street.

—a winter battle

It snowed ashes all night.
    The windows are black.
        I strap on downy armour
        slowly over bruised shoulders,
    and rattle up the stairs,
to shove the storm door open.

        Brandishing my shovel,
    I greave through deep drifts,
follow half-buried
footprints to where you
    struggled up the bank
            and left in a taxi.

A distant snow blower
    coughs up the ruins
        of a hard-fought night.
        To forget the tightness in my jaw,
    I haul back the shovel and stab
into dense mounds,

            curse it up and across
    the roof of your car.
Blowback stings me through
gaps in my visor.
    Should I call you? No.
            Maybe you've texted.

No. Maybe you thumbed,
I'm coming home now,
and forgot to hit *Send.*
Maybe you are vexed.
My phone on vibrate,
I tuck it between
my wrist and my glove.

Before waking, I dreamed
of ten-car pile-ups, planes
circling, lives changed forever.
I dig harder, clearing
the driveway at last.
Dust clings to my blade.

The ashes keep coming.
All flights are grounded.
Emergency crews
plough buried side streets,
reconnect power.
Then my glove vibrates and
in my hurry to get the phone

it slips to the sidewalk, skitters
into the street just in time
for a plough
to bury it. I find a cave among
the new mounded boulders, slip
into the muffled quiet,
renounce my anger and
curl up to wait for the thaw.

—flurries

in your frigid gaze
each breath becomes a snowstorm
over the mountain

—high anxiety in red head cove

for Greg and Erinn

A frozen cascade   in the shadow of the cliff   locks gravity
inside stalactites, broken bundles of bones   some stained
brown   by the slow trickle that mocks my memory   of this
waterfall.   I've come to play, to defy the thaw.   And never
wonder, *Why?*   To be one with the breath?   Whatever that
means.   To find my edge?   Is that enough?   I retighten my
boot laces,   snap on cleats   and where the icefall meets the
beach,   pause to press the icepicks to my lips.

The blades chip the ice face once, twice,   each time I inch
higher.   Each time tiny shards splinter around me.   I rest
my cheek against the ice,   and for a moment   I'm grafted to
this element   even as a large bundle breaks away,   falling
silent   until it smashes into surf below.

Reborn, I am cradled in the cliff's shadow   as one of its own.
It's a communion,   foundation enough just to keep climbing.
As the sun breaks the ridge,   ice surrenders somewhere inside.
The cold face shifts and I look up   to the unattainable ridge.
Meltwater mingles with tears.

February on Lawlor's Brook

Beneath a balsam fir near the footbridge
A huddled wraith shivers in the snow.
Between her fingers, a cigarette's red glow.
Her breath billows into the stillness, merges
With moonless starlight. In contemplation
Of the heavens her head tilts back. I search
For reasons to explain my timid approach.
A gust of love for this apparition
Shoves me down beside my daughter's crutches,
My arm slides gentle around her flight feathers,
And I feel her edge, this waif. Just hold her.
Just let her go. Forget all those who judge.
As we lean together, I understand
I must find the courage to be her friend.

—february/march falafel

for Kathleen Winter and her old guitar

Let not lone lunching on a bleak winter day see you forgo
a garnish!
Let not solemn clouds in a low-hung sky sap joy from a
sprig of green.
You see your face upside down, suspended in a teaspoon
stirring
Syrian lemon into your tea, knowing this is the saddest
you've ever been.

Let not grieving bones bound in a shawl keep you from
savouring summer.
Let not headlines, where they lie beside your plate, steal
your truth.
Put a smile on your fork, forget where your lovers might
be, or how deep
lie the roots that leave you restless and lunching alone in
your booth.

—changing channels

Sit with me on the couch tonight and see
How trust is betrayed in a merciless game.
Watch lives undone in the camps of refugees.

In news footage from a rock-strewn alley
Planes barrel bomb hospitals. Who's to blame?
Sit with me on the couch tonight and see

Children who are stripped from their families,
Are lost behind wire fences, mired in shame,
Their lives undone in the camps of refugees.

Hauled from the tide they become nobody,
Slouching in long lines, reciting their names.
Come sit on the couch with me now and see

How they are all pushed slowly to their knees
But somehow find the will to tend the flame.
Whose lives are undone in the camps of refugees?

We mistake scars from their fight to be free
For nightly news and 15 minutes' fame.
Sit by me on the couch tonight and see
Our lives undone in the camps of refugees.

—fighting for father

His voice jabs me in the ribs, a blunted foil:
Keep your guard up.
          Wait. Wait.
          Move your feet.
To this day I still wonder what he wanted

from us as we learned to dance with pain,
fighting those brothers of mine in the basement.
          Wait,
          punch. Punch!
His words, hardboiled, dizzying as his knuckles

to this day. And my hands in thick gloves clasping
a collar or torn sleeve to pull a body towards and under me.
          Lunge, upper cut.
          Head thudding
door frames. And knees. No room to grapple

or throw the clincher. But I see now,
          the chafed and reddened faces,
          my young brothers crying.

—song in february

What do willows know?   That the time has come?   The
nights are still so cold that the day's sun-thawed puddles
crystalize overnight into delicate sheets of ice that shatter
hollow underfoot. At dawn snow is a thin blanket   on a
lonely bed.

Nothing moves   except the brook   and a gang of crows
working the neighbourhood.   Two months more before
dandelions roar.   But along the river   mop-headed choirs
emerge   from willow buds bursting with a chorus   of
woods and meadows and hope.

March on Lawlor's Brook

Their new buds sticky in the freeze and thaw,
Spruce, balsam fir, beech, oak, chestnut and cherry, —
Roots freed from cold plastic nurseries—
Ten springs growing, reawaken to draw
Winter's thinning blood into greening shoots.
I planted them on the south bank of the brook
To one day shade the pools for trout and hook,
Where two children splash and a duck objects.
I dread the approaching fall of my decay,
Yet marvel at that fear when a satellite
Traces across the dusk a thin pathway
And then vanishes into spectral night.
Grandchildren's children may forget grandpop,
But I pray wading shadows never stop.

—electric and falling

Every single flake forms around an electrostatic speck of dust, Florence hollers over her shoulder   and steers into the maelstrom.

So, without dust, no snow?

I suppose so, she says.   *Dust   static.*

So, no clouds?   Without electricity?

Question for another day, she says.

It's Easter Saturday,   before the sun flares on the horizon, and with my keeper, I am riding to the old Wolf Brook heliport.   Then, near the Gaff drumlin on Old Track Road, the air crackles   and we are bathed in a blue halo.   The wall of white collapses and the sky surrounds us   on an ocean of snow, three months thick,   that smothers lichened grey granite and berries   blue as blood.

She opens the throttle and we surge ahead. Behind us, a trail of apparitions.

—a cold case

In memory of B.F.

A schoolboy chasing his soccer ball found the body
in the woods behind the mental hospital. Half buried, cold,
fetal, failed by a world that could never just let you pass.
A coroner examined the scars from how we abandoned you,
declared a heart-attack and exposure in the snow.
Two weeks dead. Soon to be ashes in the family plot.

We last met in the frozen section at the market. *There is a plot*
against me, you told me. *Somebody*
wants me dead, you whispered while I held a bag of frozen snow
peas in my hands. Your eyes wide with cold
dread, and as paranoid as you seemed to me, you
foretold your shallow grave. I downplayed it, *This'll pass.*

There's a way through it. My hand on your worn fall jacket, I
passed
over the strain in your voice. *It's a plot*,
you said again. *I can't go back to the shelter, not now*, you
said. *Something bad happened there but nobody*
believes me, you said. *But I can't remember what it was.* I
wanted to scold
you, cousin, but your clenched knuckles know

you need shelter. Sheilagh's Brush is coming. 15 centimetres
of snow.
Where can you go? Do your sisters still live beyond the overpass?
Grown children? Your ex-wife? I asked.
Let's not open a cold

case, you said. We laughed. Your life was a line I couldn't plot.
I just wanted somebody else to help you, anybody.
So instead of offering real help, I asked where I could drive
you.

We climbed into the van and I asked again what I could do.
But I was useless. I lied to myself. I spewed words, a snow
screen, feigned empathy, while I fought every intuition in my
body
to let you sleep for one night at my house, withheld a repast
of sympathy and instead gave my best Judas-smile and joined
the plot.
I smiled, *Yes* meaning, "Be hungry." I said, *Take this*, meaning,
"Be cold."

You wanted to talk but I jabbered on to stop you cold.
As we drove, I recalled the winter I lived with your
family, you
played trumpet, your parents were both alive. Each second a
point in the plot line
to the mall on the other side of town. Wipers smeared flakes
of snow.
I slipped you a twenty and pointed to the food court. Your
impassive,
Thanks for the ride, is still with me. No blame. I was
nobody.

See you later. No wake for your body, just a small gathering in
your memory.
Driving home past the Waterford, I see kids playing
soccer near the woods.
In my garden plot I will soon plant snow peas, now that the
nights are not so cold.

—letting go

The sun's arc is steeper.   The dog pants as it stretches along the sliding door.   The old girl is a puddle in a summer road, barely lifts her head as I slip by   step out into my breath, fetch the pitchfork from the shed.   In the far corner of the yard,   I scratch at the skin of the compost   the core is still frozen.   It's too soon for seeds, but there's still time to plan the planting.   I know I won't.   Likely all tomatoes again this year.

But even as I cling to tradition, I feel the change. My hands, that once could dig all day, rebel.   I bend thumbs into their palms to stop the spasms. Rubbing my hands together   helps unclench the tendons.   What was it I meant to do?   The greying brown boxer that I call dumb as a post   sits round-eyed in the window.   Her leash dangles from her mouth.

—soup bone

in the back garden
    the dog worries a chicken bone
        inside I dream eggs

—binocular

Moments after the gunshot,
an eagle spirals ragged
out of the afternoon, veers
into the north wind,
collapses near the edge of the eyrie,
hangs a second beside the single egg,
then topples like a child's kite
from the topmost branches
to boulders
at the base of the tree.
The male, smaller, drifts close, circles
the nest. A hare dangles in its talons.

Its piercing call unanswered,
the male drops to its mate,
and after flexing and flapping its wings,
attempts with torn flesh
to rouse her.

Next week under the perch a few
feathers
is all the coyotes have left.
The male is perched high overhead
where with another cry and a show
of wings he forsakes the sky
and nestles down to spark
the warm fracturing from within.

April on Lawlor's Brook

This spring a dozen double-crested cormorants
Pitched on the river gabions and left
White fecal trails on the black sediment.
They vied for the widest shelf to nest.
They courted there for weeks but never spoke,
Never made a sound, never roused me.
Silently left the brook for the Atlantic,
An ocean wide with possibility.
Perched at this table, it's immaterial
Whether you upend a bowl of cereal,
Or whether antipsychotics ease your pain.
There's time to embrace before we abandon
This moment you and I share today
And admit the lost ties we once obeyed.

—american goldfinch

for Shawn Fitzpatrick

I hear a soft thud
    on glass, and pushing
        back from my laptop,
            I run to the sunroom window
to see the sharp-shinned hawk.

But the birch branch
    is bare. Juncos unruffled
        at the feeder, toss
            sunflower husks to the snow
where a yellow finch lies,

black wings limp
    as an old garden glove.
        Just as I turn with a sigh back to work,
            I see his legs twitch once, and again.
So I jump into boots and scramble outside.

The bird, stunned by the falling,
    plays dead for the giant who crouches
        and exhales a cloud of pity.
            I cup the bird in my hand,
marvel at its sturdy weightlessness.

If I carry him inside, the sudden heat
    or the strangeness of captivity
        might finish him. So I wait.
            The juncos stop chirping
and return to the feeder.

The wind pinches my fingers,
pokes sharp twigs up under my shirt,
and I covet my coat,
still slung on its hook in the porch;
The goldfinch flexes its wings.

His claws clutch my ring finger
as I sidle one handed
across the snow crust.
Ice crystals rake my knees.
The juncos startle again.

Under thorny branches bent low
with blackened rosehips,
I flex my hand,
but the bird will not release me,
resists my persistent nudge.

My fingers burn with cold
when the finch finally steps onto a shoot,
wavers there, holds.
I stagger inside, claw a duvet
over my shoulders, wait for flight.

—heart failure

for Chris Brookes

I'm lying, you have to believe me.

I

Let me be the battery that powers your radio.
Let me play you stories you never knew you wanted to hear.

From the last house on Battery Road,
I hear the fishing boats labouring
in Fort Amherst Basin. I hear the sea
sweep over Chain Rock
to hammer the wharves and what remains.

I wish the tide could drag my past
out through the Narrows and scuttle it
out there where it might stay true.
But I've floated all my stories so often
they no longer resemble the truth.

Whenever I repeat your name,
it comes out as static. Each syllable
acid on my tongue. I sip nettle tea
and pray for resurrection.
Mine or yours? Is there a difference?
If I blame myself for remembering,
could you love me again?

I rise in the Battery and preach
like a radio tuned to gospel,
things I didn't know God wanted me to say.
You tell me, *You sure sound good—too good—for someone*
I buried in my past.
                                        But I know the thief
who lies in wait beneath your grief. He will take everything.

II

On the deck of our 65-footer you laugh,
your fingers entangle at the back of my neck.
I wait for you to pull me towards a kiss,
but when I look up, I am back on shore.
I hear the low hum as the boat slides slowly
out along the apron and into ocean clutter.
I call to you. And you, bracing your thigh
against the gunwale, raise your hands to shout,
but I hear nothing. The wind whips your hair,
shreds your voice. I wave and you
turn your face to the sea. Sail into blue polygons.

911

Air rushes in as the needle is withdrawn from my chest.
Halleluiah. My memory is fading.
I have been saved.

—shem meditates on his disease

There is nobody in the water.   I listen to their splashing.
No one sings to me anymore.   And the songs rend my heart.
I know we are close because we never touch.   All this is
true, because it never happened.   And I remember it all.   I
practise hard to get this wrong   every time.

When shadows arise, I invite them in.   I invite them to
leave me alone.   They knit themselves a nest   and haunt
me.   They are guides to nowhere.   I am the bones   of
everything they cannot resist.

I thought only crows rested in the graves of crows.   I've
never truly understood a single event in my life.   I am certain
of that.   And if that is the end   then let it be.   I will give
you the ungiveable so you may forgive me   the unforgivable,
and then let's all go for a drowning.

—hit and run

over weak coffee
    and two glazed donuts untouched
        guilt hovers like steam

—undone

You free wild cats
from a magazine
with the scissors
you use to tame
your pubic hair,
trim threads from my underwear,
snip brown leaves from the hops.

In the dusty morning,
you ravish your desk
with the cloth
you use to soothe
the corners of my mouth,
blunt the sting of ice on a bruise.

You trace the edge
of my tattooed scar
with the same finger
you use to uncrust
your Persian's eyes,
stir honey in tepid tea,
knead yourself to the verge.

You cut through linen
to the flesh,
finger the wound, and
lick everything clean.

May on Lawlor's Brook

From farmer's son, who as a boy here played,
I learned the brook has changed course several times,
Not floods, but bulldozed as developers laid
Their pole lines, water pipes, and sewer lines.
A suspicious otter rummages here now,
And a small flock of ducks lingers year round;
In spring they attend skittish peeps of yellow
Among the rocks, nurse some to fledging brown.
We who inherit this narrow cradle herd
Our own broods along the gravel and fret
That time has not yet revealed the threat
That might steal them from us without a word.
But with each one we lose, to hawk or earth,
I learn to love the power in the plough of birth.

—Calvary

After Mary Jo Bang

The yellow stripe goes with black,   *goes with yellow, goes with*
black,   *and wings that work in practise will not work in theory.*
So says our guide.   She herds us to the almost empty apiary
near the crest of a small mound.

The one-in-every-crowd tourist raises his hand,   asks how
time waxes in the combs of the bees.   *Nervous laughter.*
The ohm of drones is alive in my chest.   The wind tilts
softly closer   through the summer-dry hay.

On I go with the other eco-tourists crowding the guide
along the green path   under the bower of almond blossoms.
The eye of a swarm approaches, swerves   and dives into the
grove of nut trees.   Surrounds the old keeper who weeps in
his netting.   We encircle him.   Someone pulls off the man's
coveralls.   He emerges white as a blanched nut.   His
hands are punctured,   his side bleeds.   *The bees are dying,*
the keeper says,   again and again.   *The bees are dying.*

Our guide laments,   *The hives will grow silent and the honey*
will harden.   The group masses around her,   everyone
hugging.   A humming from these fake bees in costume
vibrates in my torso   we all fall to our knees.   Buzz. No
Buzz.   Fallow fields are abandoned, while nearby   a drone
drone drones   from stigma to stigmata to a tower which
bears   witness in pocked letters: DRON BATT RY RE HARGER.

What's the buzz?   the tourist sings.   *Tell me what'za happenin'.*

—mother's day revisited

On the first Mother's Day after you died. I felt nothing.
Whatever was between us may have been a convenient
way for me to avoid saying, *You left me.* And you
responding, *You want too much from me.* In later years we
visited on holidays, went through all the rituals. Except, the
only Mother's Day I called was after you were diagnosed
with cancer.

You were barely twenty-four when Dad threw your clothes
onto the lawn and banished you for spreading your
legs for some married guy you both knew. You say it
didn't happen. Truth is you lugged your suitcase back
to your mother and stayed gone.

I have no childhood memories of you. There are pictures of
a park bench and you posing with me and two of my
three brothers in cowboy hats, or me buried in sand. That
is someone else's life.

Years later, you stopped to pick up a hitchhiker not
knowing it was me until I opened the door. You bought
me dinner. You took me in after I left prison and fed me
until I married and left home for another ocean. You even
came to visit once. And much later, after we moved back,
you reached out with gifts for my daughters.

I am grateful   for all of that,   and your weakness for strays.
You reached through me   to heal deeper regrets. For that I
loved you.   Enough to be there for one last muddled game of
cards,   for a last drink together,   for your last attempt at
suicide,   to ask you, *Where should we take your ashes* (that
was a mistake),   for your last breath.

There are other times, like today,   when your hand is cold
on my shoulder   and I relive every memory of you,
searching for a warm touch or a glance.   Each time I come
back empty   to this longing, and it hurts   because my
grieving is easy.

—a reason to smile

I choke on my own voice
and run into the driveway,
angry with you, angry with me,
that I let you make me spin out of control.
I feel like a knee-jerk watch dog.
I wash your clothes, mind the grandkids.
Inbound jets come roaring out of the sky.
Things could be okay.

I stub my toe on a brick someone left
in the driveway. I pick up the scooter
and the bike, hobble them into the backyard.
Everything is alright.
The garden is overgrown, grass in thick clumps.
New leaves hang frost nipped, last year's grapes
are raisins on the vine, and I realize
the weight I feel in *my* bones
is mine alone to carry.

I see a stranger in the street
with a woman on his back.
They don't know me,
but I wonder if they could tell me
why I'm laughing?

—he drank the river

It is late when the sun
melts shadows from the alley where he sleeps.
Darkness drips from the hem of his coat.
Just off downtown Yonge Street,
old Acorn gasps on the flop-house steps while
a dark rivulet stains the curb, the greasy gutter.
Not yet old, but nearly gone, he heads
for the Waverly to steady his nerves.

So many words yet to find—in this trade
that leaves him falling for alcohol, calling,
and falling, fermenting, fomenting,
taking flight along Donwood Ravine.

Lost for months now, or is it hours?
It is ten years yet before his ex-wife
will put her head in a gas oven. But before that
befalls them, he must drink himself to death.
He must put dreams to paper.
He must be here, intoxicated by his vision,
publishing mimeographs from a bunker
for young writers in every dive,
snatching anything he can steal
from bohemian embassies, fermenting, fomenting,
gnawing hollow bones.

In the alley Acorn, with adoration pooling around him,
envisions his future in a half-full glass,
a lifeline blurred by beer and memories
of hostile gunfire that punctuate his sleep.
He knows the revolution will not wait.
He knows streams are converging along the edge.

One small victory is all he needs,
        and he sees it in the tears of his acolytes,
sees the river slowly carving deeper channels.
        He christens the movement, toasts voices with alcohol.
They echo inside his hollow bones.
        He must take flight over the ravine.

        Acorn, eyes like a bird,
drags his battle feathers out
        of the alley to skirmish in the open
                flow of the sidewalk,
        into the streaming honks
                and down the street,
                        even as the concrete heaves,
                                tilts him sideways
and he pukes so hard he forgets he can fly.

From his habitual bar stool, he recalls submissions,
        staples the corners of anger and love, gives it away,
                gives away the song inside himself.
        Fuck, he is thirsty. He *is* thirst.
He drinks the river of his pain. He is fermenting,
fomenting for the people.
        And their song
                lifts him out of himself.

June on Lawlor's Brook

The pools green with weeds, and the water seeps
Over the rocks and fills this tributary,
Carrying seeds and mosquito larvae deep
In dark, mirrored clouds rising from the wary
East. They are coming, and we grow weary
And slow in the heat, forget to keep
Faith with the widening commentary
Where this brook and Virginia River meet.
And so, I fear, I've drifted through my days
And let the thoughts that carry me sweep me
Away. Just now I sensed the quickening
Of early summer rain, when nothing stays
As it is for long before rushing free
Down river, to the sea of awakening.

—coming clean

In the shower, warm water
pours over my head and chest.
I'm stepping out of my skin.

Becoming droplets. Becoming that river.
Do you remember how we lay there?
Arms bent in the coolness, seeking
speckled trout where they hid
underneath the banks. Rubbing fingertips
along smooth bellies, I grabbed for the gills,
flung fish thrashing into the grass.
You always wanted to put them back.

The shower drums my ribs,
a torrent of rain that patters a pool.
Near the bank, two cranes wade, necks long
and supple, arms intertwined, their beaks
imitating hands. I want to reach out,
hold you close, but I so often failed
when you needed me, that now
I'm afraid we're too far apart.

The water trails down my back
and licks the inside of my thighs.
The rivulets converge
at my feet and I am reminded
of our last hike together.
You spied a newborn calf, and then
its mother, her head immersed
among pond lilies. Returning for air,
she was startled by our closeness and gave chase.
I raced you all the way back to the car.

Naked now on these cold tiles
I am ready for my confession.

—amy chains

Lyrics: Wade Kearley
Music: Tamsyn Russell

Never had no other lover could get inside my head.
My face is crying in the mirror when I remember what you did

Chorus

You took a taxi to the station, you boarded a one way train.
Now I feel so damn broken, I just can't stand the pain

Chorus

It meant nothing that I loved you, love's chains are all I get.
They're wound so tight around me, that I never can forget

Chorus

These heavy drag down blues, got me chained up every day
and I never saw it coming, until I saw you walk away

Outro
Oh yeah Amy, Amy, Amy, I said Amy unchain me.
Go on set me free.
Tell me what I need to hear
go on Amy unchain me.
Set me free

—and now that you are not there

If I could see you tonight, we'd sit in the car,
rain hitting the sunroof, the windows ajar,
admitting the mist, a hint of grass
laden with pollen and dust from fallow fields.

I might bring tulips or white and purple lilacs,
or perhaps the peppery lupine plucked
along the path. I might not bring you flowers
at all. I might bring honey. I might bring
an emergency roadside flashlight. I might bring
a hymn torn from your book of songs.

I might caress your feet, press my fingers
between your toes, imagine anything was
possible. Our gossip, weeds in a greenhouse,
stalky and tangled, impatient for sunlight.

Alone as the sun bows the horizon,
sleep forgotten, I recall the promises forsaken,
the vanity that permitted my betrayals.
And as my needs slowly untangle, I pray
for the flicker of a songbird
and the moment when desires take flight.

—postcard from the hills above clarenville

The morning glowers as I shiver up through the dawn.   Birds chatter in the trees,   thunder tumbles.   In the narrow clear-cut, fog scours tree stumps,   dampens piles of blasty branches with a heavy mist.   The wind combs blackflies into my hair.   I hurry on under the brow of the storm, knowing deerflies will sniff me out if I stop   for a breath, knowing I have a hundred miles   and miles more, before I shed the weight on my back.

I try to think only of where I am   right now.   Let the distance take care of itself,   one step at a time. And in this hush   thoughts of family—of my sweet daughters darting barefoot   through their youth.

And now, the crackle all around   as lightning   rips the morning open.   I feel a nudge from each of the people who shared their homes and lives with me   for a laugh, a meal, a night.   My home is five days' hike away,   but tonight there will be refuge   under another stranger's roof.

July on Lawlor's Brook

Kneeling, I found a frog in my tomato patch,
Hidden there under the protective scrim
As summer forgot to deepen and the frog to swim.
As it bobbed in the bucket that I'd fetched,
I vowed it would not die under my watch,
This soft-skinned prayer. Grandchildren on a whim
Decided they knew what was best and fed him
Crackers on his plank boat, then went to dredge
Worms and black beetles from the river mud.
Cold blooded, I pondered the lost years I took
Worshipping in my garden as if it were a nave,
Me wholly hidden, harrumphing like a dud.
And so, I sloshed the bucket to the brook,
Decanted the only hymn that I could save.

—postcard from under a bridge

The thumb-sized beetle   shoves its brown body from the
brook and climbs a boulder,   clings there, pushing and
shoving   at the husk of its underwater life.   New flesh
emerges, emerald shingles   and the shimmer of transparent
wings.   It waits there, buffeted,   gathering all the wind
can tell.   Wings turn like antennae   sensing every draft,
unfold,   flicker   as its colours fade to black.   Almost torn
from the rock   by the wind, it climbs slowly   to a smooth
lip of granite and,   its lessons at an end,   the dragon flies.

—*il cauto*

(study for a documentary on the secret life of squid)

She jets away from her squad,
her three hearts all pumping copper blood,
then she darts through my breath as it worries upward.
Her tentacles drift over her funnel and mantle,
then trail in streamers as she circles me,
pulsing red. In a cloud of blue ink
she dives upward to glide briefly
into the air, then returns to the sea.
She cloaks herself once more in blue, but her fear
dissolves when a school of small fish sprints by.
She snags one with a tentacle and deftly drags
the herring fry into her arms,
subdues it with toxins that kindle its heart.
She shreds its flesh with her beak
and then flies away. Her wing-like fins
beat as she descends, avoiding my slow-motion pans
that would record her secret life. I trail her
into twilight, her mantle dotted by glowing pins
as she flees the focus of my attention,
retreats into the crush of blackness
where she is the only source of light.
Her skin red, then pink, then grey, until
I switch the floodlights on. Then her mantle
bloats, and she propels herself so rapidly
she vanishes. Distance is her camouflage
as she skirts back to join the countless, swarming
upward. These shape-shifters choreograph a hunger
beyond my imagination, a dance of desires
that I may behold but can never possess.

—*il audace*

(a swimming-pool video)

In my search online for swimming pools,
I discovered a crucifixion on Vimeo.
Under the water she kicks in rough circles
while bubbles trail from one nostril. A rope
of hair uncoils over her shoulder as she ascends
into the eye of her reflection. A breath
and she returns, flying, falling backwards
into the camera. The muscles of her long back,
buttocks, thighs, fill my field of vision.
Suspended in her element she scissors
legs that could crush me, splays toes
along her calf, then crosses her knees. She hovers,
arms outstretched, her spinning torso
unwinds into a simple kick. Another breath
and then straight down. Her silhouette glides
forever beyond my imagining.
She sinks calmly to the bottom of the pool,
pulls knees to her chin, then dolphins upward,
into her mirror image at pool edge and vanishes
—until I hit *Replay* and
feel her inside me once again.

—winter island

for Michael Winter, who tipped me off

On the west side of this
Northwest Atlantic island—
part African,
part Appalachian,
part earth's mantle,
shoved to the surface
before there were glaciers—
on the west side of this island
is a long lake, Wli'Qospem
or Grand Lake to the settlers.

To satellites it is an exclamation
one hundred kilometers,
north to south, dammed, wired.
And in that lake at the southern end
is an island, the eighteenth largest
lake island in the world.
Glover's Island we call it now.
And on Glover's Island lie many ponds,
all unnamed except the few like
Kettle, Quartz, and Tomahawk,
named by prospectors
who, even now, drill cores for gold.

On that island
in the North Atlantic in
Grand Lake, on
Glover Island in

one of those nameless ponds, is
a nameless island
the size of two ice rinks,
spruce clinging to the south end,
Labrador tea to the north.

And on that nameless island is
a seasonal gully that fills with
ice melt and early rain.
And in that gulley on
that unnamed island in
that nameless pond on
Glover's Island in
Grand Lake on
the west side of that island rises
a sod of peat in which is rooted
an alder bush.

It is the smallest wildland
ever found, this alder
clinging to a sod island in
a gulley on an island
in a pond on an island
in a lake on that Afrilachian island
in the cold Northwest Atlantic.

—every calipitter in the whole galaxy

A serious bit of nonsense for Annika and every other kid who ever re-invented a word.

Could god create a word so long and so heavy
There was no way she could hoist all the letters?
Would there be enough room in the whole galaxy?

Imagine a tree with so many leaves
They grew all too fast for the world's calipitters.
Could she not create so leafy a tree?

Imagine the silk cocoon they might weave,
So vast it could hide the Milky Way in its net,
The biggest room in the whole galaxy.

What if each day was a day to be free?
Would beaches be packed if we never vacate?
Does god have a word for so lengthy a day?

Imagine a big whale that bungs up the sea.
When it slaps its tail, would we all get wet?
Would nothing be dry in the whole galaxy?

Whenever I sing the song that I sing it tastes salty.
The taste is so strong that I can't forget
God yet might create a word that's soooo lengthy
It would sop up every letter in the whole g a l   a   x   y

August on Lawlor's Brook

In my larch-shade hammock, an infant clutched
Under my arm, I dreamt we swam up river
Into a concrete cavern where fins touched.
Schooling with brown trout we shared a fever
For headwaters beyond the culvert's reach.
There, like Shanawdithit and her mother,
Last of their kind, we yielded on a sandy beach
To forces from which we would not recover.
Slowly, for the last time, we turned our backs
On the marshes and birch groves and beseeched
Merciless strangers to let us go back
To our watery hiding places. Flushed,
I woke to sunburned cheeks and the hammock
Above me and the baby gone forever.

—postcard
from the holiday inn

Last night a bus load of them landed late,   laughing, doors slamming.   I drag my hand across the blanket, tiny static sparks.   My first night in a real bed after days on the trail. The memory of unseen birds singing   lingers at night like a half-remembered tune.   Through the patio door   warm night air drifts in with a trace of diesel.   The roar of a truck on the bypass   becomes rain on the flysheet.   Tires on a wet street below my window   become the wind through the forest.   The distant thud of rock and roll   becomes my heartbeat.   I see the silhouette of treetops and the sky behind.   The caw of street kids   becomes the dawn call of a crow: *Go! Go! Go!*   My calves ache.

—living in the night sky

I hear the zephyr mutter to the stars,
The old man's come back to sleep for an hour
In his hammock, lolling under the larch.

Why come so often? What is in his heart
To lie still for so long under the boughs?
I hear the zephyr mumble to the stars.

In stars, the ancients read destiny's art,
But omens are just meteor showers
To him as he lounges under the larch.

Perhaps the lovers are drifting apart
So he retreats to this private bower?
I hear the zephyr murmur to the stars.

I think it's simply, "we are who we are,
Until we aren't." He's not dodging arrows—
To lounge in the hammock under the larch—

He's looking to finish what he started.
The old man's come back to sleep for an hour,
I hear the west wind murmur to the stars,
From my hammock waking beneath the larch.

—argument with my heart

At my feet a jellyfish
amid the mid-summer ribbons of kelp.
No pulse, no thought, no bones,
as the swish of the tide
scours its grave.

I chide two children who would scoop it up,
who would hold the milky galaxy in a plastic lid,
and carry it dripping to the picnic table,
tugging blue flies into orbit.

The stinging tentacles ripple in the backwash
as the dome of the evening slides down.
With a discarded plastic shovel, I prod this alien
into the retreating tide, until it shifts, then lifts
and then begins to float away.

I am stranded by the thought:
What need has it to follow
my plan? The ocean is its heart,
the moon its thoughts. And for bones?
For bones, it has this gravel strand.

September on Lawlor's Brook

The wind-loving kestrel hovers then drops
And quickly flaps its pointed wings, lifts
A captured frog into a birch, alights,
Pins with talons until the kicking stops.
Krill, krill, it calls its mate and unwraps
Sinew from bone in this month of plenty
With chicks long flown and, even in this heat,
Prepares for the cold days when birdsong stops.
I know it is coming, and I must be prepared.
In the midst of plenty I reach for you
And come back empty, my talons laid bare.
I ask myself, "What more could I say or do?"
You can't dig deep for feelings that aren't there.
Love's sharp beak shreds me. I must start anew.

—splitting wood

Birch, wild cherry, maple, spruce and balsam fir   lie in a jumbled heap.   Wood I scrounged in the aftermath   log by log from backyards, abandoned meadows,   anywhere the hurricane felled it.   I chainsawed each one into luggable lengths,   dumped it here.

The nights are getting colder now.   I need a fire to drive away regret for summer's passing.   I've reached the end of my procrastination,   but with axe in hand I hesitate.   I no longer swing the blade in expectation   that the wood will split as I intend.   Now wary of the grain,   I carefully prep each junk before I strike.

First on the block, the cherry.   One hand balances the junk on end,   the other touches metal to the sweet spot.   Axe slowly up,   and down with both hands hard on the handle. The wood grabs   and holds the blade.   I raise the axe again. Again.   And again,   until the junk yields into slats clinging by thick fibers   I cannot pry apart.

There's a shot of sun across the lot.   You're smiling through the kitchen window,   and I wonder when I last opened up to you after thirty years.   What would I say?   Never something to debate,   to agree or agree to disagree.   We sleep in the same bed.

Next, two pale planes of maple leap away from the blade.   A second one splits, and a third.   Then the axe jams in a long spruce junk.   Once. Twice.   I drive the crack deeper,

wider.   Did we merge that way before our betrayals?   Did
the cordage hold? Even as we were riven?   On the back deck
you shield your eyes   and raise an imaginary cup to your
lips.   The birch will wait.

—the divorce of aurora borealis

At dawn a herd of caribou stampedes
across the tattooed slope of your left thigh
as you kick me from under the woolen blanket.

You yawn and gather the folds.
With your arm newly etched in fire,
you banish me. You remind me how
last night I failed you when I refused

to dance beneath your North Star.
Alone, you began with arms overhead,
summoned spirits from the constellations.
They spread like oil on water,
aflame with their voyage to the afterlife.
I stood staring skyward, mouth agape.

This morning is too early to forget,
too late for regret. I unzip the tent flap,
stick my head outside, breathe vapors
into the early light. The air is electric
and I scurry from under canvas
as you roll to one knee.
Your cough shakes the ground.

The propane hisses and the kettle
sputters with Labrador tea,
brewed to bargain for forgiveness.
But for you, the rivers of Hudson's Bay

would not slake your thirst. You stumble
in stockinged feet across the lichen and rubble,
heading northward.
Your capote crackles with static.

—from under our blanket

Under our disaster blanket,   your arm with the tattooed number lies heavy across my chest.   Canvas shivers in the northeast breeze,   new snow clogs the ditches,   hunger nicks my bones.   Under the illusion that   freedom is a right,   we married, built our house in hope.   Tonight, the bane of hope helicopters overhead.   Our whispers are distorted under the arc of a searchlight.   We are cast away, cold   with nothing in our cup   except a meagre sip of desperation.

I dreamed a child   cocooned in the darkest corner of this hovel   singing us home,   helping us forgive and heal.   Can we dream her into being?

When I pull you trembling close   I can feel how far I am adrift   from who I want to be for you.   Light glints through a slit, and I barely recognize your eyelids swollen,   lips split, but your breathing is familiar, long and slow.   Your legs soften under my thigh,   and I kiss your salt-lick shoulder. Before I can surrender   once more you breathe promise into my life.

—the words of the moon

After Ai Ch'ing's "The Words of the Sun"

If I blunt the fall of night,   will you let me see her bruised
face?   Let me bathe her with light   as she lies in your arms
among the eelgrass?   You escaped the life you expected,
drifted too quickly into the river of desire,   then lost
yourself and the life you wanted,   as the dark rapids stole
everything to which you clung.

Startled by the pain,   the first drop of blood,   you called
to me   and I brought you rebirth in the flood,   a narrow
cradle, the river's gift.

Water strokes the bank where you pull the raft ashore.
A fragrant smoke drags through spruce.   The sun returns
with its infinite patience.   Love betrays its promises,   but I
will renew them.   I know how a lie   can cut deep.   And I
know how rebirth can heal.

—tea & bread rising

I

Sugar and yeast, water and flour. Salt
spilled on the counter. After a night
of baking, the stove
purrs quiet with birch embers.

I linger in the dawn and break the first crust,
drain the pot. There is time
before I must leave. I lift the sash and whistle
for the finch in the gooseberry bush.

II

I watch the light
descend Nord Hill
one last time,
feel my hand quake. Surf
torn by the headland.
Your memory retreats
with the darkness
on this morning
of reckoning.
I fumble into gaiters.

III

Sugar and yeast, water and flour. Salt spilled
in the cooling kitchen. The loaves soften
under their sheen of butter.

I shove one last junk into the stove,
wash a crust down with the dregs,
then slap my cup and saucer against the hearth.
In the porch, the first rays ignite steamed glass.
My coat wrapped tight around me,
I go out to greet the undertow.

—full moon over wreck cove

This hard rock in its woolish coat of brown and green
shelters houses along the lane, odd buttons sewn into the
    slate.
I crouch among the thick alders, halfway up the hill and,
protected from the north winds,
watch broken surf as it scrambles over itself
in the gut, tears away at the seams.
I button my swileskin and wonder,
Am I unravelling too?
Why do I deserve this dream?

October on Lawlor's Brook

Brushing my teeth in the darkened bathroom,
I glimpse through the upstairs window a silhouette
That stealthily scales the fence—my love exhumed.
Face to cool glass, I watch it limp moonlit
Towards the house and disappear beneath
The eave until twisted hands grab hold,
Drag its skeleton up onto the porch,
Eyes pleading as it shivers in the cold.
Morning fills my bed with light and I'm free.
The remains of last night's dying storm
Fill the swollen brook with raging memories
That roil against the footbridge, dirt-brown foam.
In the garden, broken limbs, leaves scattered wet.
What will it take for you, for me, to forget?

—crucifying corey

What were you thinking when you kicked in my
basement door? When you rifled my medicine cabinet? What
were you thinking when I came home too soon and you
leapt out my bedroom window! Corey? Did you
think I'd make a victim impact statement and forget I
ever saw you? That I'd hide my jewellery in a bucket
behind the furnace, nail all the windows secure
forever and ever and ever amen?
That I'd tell all my daughters to bar all the doors
whenever they took a shower?

I'll bet you never expected
the cops to tell *me your* name, *your* address,
send *me your* mugshot, then
wash their hands of you.

And you damn well never expected
me at your father's door with a stud-finder,
four-inch nails and a pneumatic hammer.
You never expected to be
splayed on the floor under your mother's cross,
You little motherfucker!
Tell me, how are your hands by the way—
Would you like a little vinegar on that?

I'm gonna feed your steroids
to tomcats and tie them in a bag
over your head and then wait
for your confession,

which I will record, in good faith,
painstakingly,
with my left hand.

—first frost

Evenings, before it arrives, the air smells of it—
a cool burning that promises hail and smouldering.

At this moment it is soft. Or the edge, at least, is blunted.
For a breath and then another it even feels as if it might turn
back.

But with the reluctant sunrise, as greys thaw into light,
and the constellations fade among the newly

bared branches of the maples,
I imagine how even the hurried rodents

tuck themselves among the grass and twine
and plastic that they knit into the roots,

and slip eagerly into torpor.

—starlings

who are the soldiers
    marching along the top of the fence
        their bones are hollow

—back to the land of the living

for Sergeant Thomas Ricketts
and in memory of Great Uncle Walter Kearley #552

Stinking mud,
and rats stealing rations, or worse, up and down the trench
while each bomb burst hammers us back.
We huddle, some crying for their mother, craving rest,
dead centre in a valley of shrapnel. We are cartographers
of fear, unnerved and hard-wired.

Bandaged flesh swells green after the wire
slashes limbs, the sharp edge of panic. We dine on mud,
mustard gas and horse flesh a la carte.
We die every day, crying for lovers or cursing the trench
mouth of politicians, or—if by luck we wrest
another day from fate—we pray to make it back

to the land of the living. I tried crawling back
once and bled my thighs on razor wire.
A dying soldier prayed for me to stay, to rest,
but two medics dragged me out of that muddle
past stark faces in the zigzagged trench
and stitched me up before I escaped on the cripple cart.

Two weeks ago we marched quick time behind that cart,
believing the Hun would soon show us their backs.
We've been turned inside out since then in these trenches.
This morning I saw the man next to me, as he read a wire

from home, erupt in a splatter of mud
and flesh, and the rest.

We crawled into his warm crater, wrestling
with broken anger and a hunger to kill, a manic art
that filled me with a dark light. I smudged a mask of mud
and, after a spray of bullets drove us back,
I charged, firing my Lewis from the hip. Wired
on fear, I captured the gunners' nest above the trench.

There's a future me they'll call hero of the trenches.
But I'm the golem of that man, will never let him rest.
There is no prescription he can write to rewire
the memories that throw screaming bodies cartwheeling
into a no-man's land where I dodged the blowback,
with only my tobacco to calm me in that labyrinth of mud.

News-reel trenches haunt me, but I try to rest as the cart carries
the "boy-hero" through the mud and my name speeds on the wire,
summons ships and newsmen, carries me back to fame and to deadlines.

—ore pony

We are not in the business of iron ore. Whatever captive iron ore sources we have, we use it to make steel.

Lakshmi Mittal

With a heart of two
fists together clenched,
the pony hauled uncounted
trollies through laboured
veins so deep beneath the bay
they took a decade to exhume.

Until one day she
slipped the halter,
galloped deeper,
past the sump pumps,
down the tunnels under
Conception Bay.

She ran in darkness,
crashing into ledges
searching caverns
for memories of blue.

Silent now, the pumps
rust as seawater rises,
ensuring her bloodline
ends in legend.

When this pony slept,
did she dream
of ovens melting iron?
Or did she dream of
a herd unshod and restless
under the steel light of the moon?

—kneeling on cranberries

It's like love, you said. *Even when you know*
where to look, you never know
what you will find, until you get there.

You led me along treacherous cliffs
to the edge of a marsh that sloped steeply
to the rocks. We clung to shrubs
as their roots dripped into tidal pools choked
with decaying seaweed and plastic scrap.
Reckless between the sunlight and the damp
that darkened the knees of your jeans, we probed
for red berries, white beneath.
They fell into the moss at the slightest touch.
By mid-morning, tired from stooping
along the verge, we found an alcove of rocks,
lay quiet, the sky propped on wet knees.
Spray from the lunar surf left a hint
of salt on fingers stained by the picking.
The earth shuddered against my back.
The thin warmth of a fall sun massaged me.
But your kiss was flat and as cold as the season.
It was then the wind swung north
and drove us back towards our lives.
Raw berries rattled in the bucket.

A month later I discover it
behind the shed door, peel off the lid,
and find your breath fragrant in my mouth.

—after wrestling with gabriel

for Des Walsh

Stripped to the waist he turns his back to the crowd,
straps on his guitar. The bar room fills with gasps
as onlookers gape at the wing stubs
protruding from under his shoulder blades.

When he faces the crowd, the stage light
reveals a fresh scar over his left ear.
He strikes the strings, spits holy disdain
and, in the lyrics of his savagery, admits
the angels have forgotten the crippled ones
who huddle in the veins of the city
injecting the drugs that make sirens cry.

His song is a curse, and a lament for the collapse
of love. From chipped tables around the pallet
where he makes his stand, the audience
smokes and burps sour hops. They drag names
from their phones until their gossip merges
with his voice and no one hears anyone else.

As each patron tumbles past the stage and out
into the street, he salutes them with a slap
on the strings. How he raves! This clipped angel.

—the poem speaks back

I

You come prowling the keyboard,
a coyote savaging the edge of a clear-cut.
What do you want from me? To lose
the fears that growl in your throat?
Or just to hear me sigh your name?

I'm not your talons, but I can hunt you.
I'm not aflame, but I can burn you.
I am your vision before you envision it.

II

Don't look for me in the fire that singes your sleeve
but never touches you.

Don't look for me in the smoke above snapping boughs
and curling bark.

Your anger at my absence is
your wounded self-pity.

It keeps me at bay, as you stumble
into the stark night.

—once when i was drowning

The bedroom window ajar on this warm October night,
thc hem of the curtain ebbs and flows.

Rain carries me away. I trace your spine with rough fingers
that smell of the tide line.

The wind swerves over the sill, rain-drenched, softly molds
the blankets, washes soft curves,

lingers in the gaps and abruptly draws back, trails seaweed,
buoyant and slack,

leans into the next wave without striving for current,
for eddy, for retreat.

Early morning, the wind turns cold. So you slip out of bed,
wade slowly to the window.

You return and we embrace, as you whisper to me of a dream
entangled by the vivid sea.

I am a near-drowned sailor whose foot finds sand.
I kiss your wet hand.

—deciduous

A persistent cawing from the top of a pole   returns me to the
moment.   I scan the sky for the osprey.   But the crows,
with their rookery in the nearby grove of spruce,   harried it
away.

Rusty chimes hanging under the larch   were silent all
summer,   but clatter now as the wind swings north.
Yellow needles rain down. One low branch heavy with
cones   chafes the fence railing,   protests again and again.

                    I rest
          on the garden bench and study
this wormy plot   that I've replenished to plunder
   year after year.

In the distance a dog   cannot keep the season at bay. Leaves
curl and sink   into the unmown lawn.   Vapors waft from
the compost pile   that soon must sleep.   A blue fly
on my muddy boot   evaporates in a blink. Black against a
blue-gray rock,   a spider
                    crawls sluggishly into October.
          The ornate tongues of frost-burned clematis
seem to say:
          What good
is the purple I know when it comes so late?

On the few remaining tomato vines,   draped over wire
frames   brown leaves falter in the wind.   The sun is a wry
smile   on each shiny globe—green, yellow, orange.   Clouds
chase the sun southward.   Above this ragged order, higher
clouds   smear   gray on white on blue.
                              A crow
                                        battles the wind and dives
                                                    into the black tangle of boughs.

—re: the last one in the sequence

found poem in email from Cynthia O'Toole

This last sonnet made me cry.
So happy that you finished.
I'm eager to hear about the process
and how you felt along the way.

I'm absolutely exhausted
from going around Nanjing,
although it was very interesting,
and I enjoyed the trip.

Woke at 7:30, my first morning
back to workmen drilling
into concrete in the next apartment.
Apparently, this will continue
until I leave.

Went to my classroom today
(only quiet place)
and slept all afternoon. Can still barely
keep my eyes open.
The heat and humidity are killing me.

November on Lawlor's Brook

Rising from dreamtime, I descend creaking
Stairs to the couch, pull back a curtain aglow
With street light. The cuckoo three times repeating.
Most birds, except the junco and the crow,
Have left the path, the brook, the brown meadow
And the road, littered now with the scratch of leaves.
All my life words were my armour. I vowed to go
When bodhrans and war cries called to rally.
But duty cannot be stitched on my sleeves.
It is here, my heart—four walls that hum with warmth.
And these words, now, soft wings for second thoughts.
I feel them hug my shoulders, calming me.
In honeycombs hidden beneath the eaves,
Bees fade slowly into silence and ease.

—on the road to mount abu

for Katherine

Overhead a skein of large-winged geese
plummet from high clouds. They honk gently,
slide into their reflection on Lake Nakki.

As shadows cool, I inhale the orchid
evening and reminisce. Your hair tumbled
in grey curls around my face. We kissed.

You left me at the terminal clutching
my suitcase on the pavement. We never
really said goodbye. Now, on the other side

of the planet,
            other side of a year, I search
your last gestures in memory, rewind
your last words for a sign. Was I asleep?

I realize the geese are all around me.
They lift white heads, turn dark eyes
towards me and flock to their feet. I freeze,

anxious not to disturb them, and breathe
a chant I learned in Udaipur:
Om mani padme hum. The geese

trill softly and push into the lake.
Moments later they are airborne. I am complete
and retrace my steps along the pathway back.

WADE KEARLEY is the author of seven other books, including the poetry collections *Drawing on Water* and *Let Me Burn like This*, and the travel books *The People's Road* and *The People's Road Revisited*, based on his 900-kilometer trek along Newfoundland's abandoned rail line. He lives in St. John's.